THE FOUR YEAR CAREER®

YOUNG LIVING EDITION

HOW TO MAKE YOUR DREAMS OF FUN & FINANCIAL FREEDOM COME TRUE

OR NOT ...

RICHARD BLISS BROOKE

ISBN 978-0-692-01987-0
Published by Bliss Business, LLC
1875 North Lakewood Drive
Coeur d'Alene, Idaho 83814
Telephone 855.480.3585
Printed in the United States of America

ABOUT THE AUTHOR
RICHARD BLISS BROOKE

In 1977, I was working at Foster Farms, the single largest chicken processing plant in the world. With only 36 years to go until retirement, I decided to change course; and at the age of 22, I joined the ranks of the Network Marketing profession. It took me three years to make a living at it. I quit many times my first year and watched thousands quit who joined before, during, and after me.

Then I figured something out—and three years later, I had 30,000 active partners building the business with me. Sure, people still failed and quit, but 30,000 people stuck with it. I was earning $40,000 a month in 1983 at the age of 28.

I figured out how to make Network Marketing work.

Thirty-six years later, I have seen thousands of companies come and go and hundreds of thousands of hopeful Distributors quit before they made it ... or maybe they would have never made it. I have seen our profession dirty its pants with its own greed, selfishness, immaturity, and general lack of character.

Primarily, the reputation of the profession has been created by the hype ... the empty promises and manipulation toward making a lot of income quickly for not a lot of effort ... and a deception about what the opportunity is all about. For decades, prospects would ask if what the sales reps were talking about was Network or Multi-Level Marketing, and the sales reps would go to great lengths to convince them it was not. It was NOT like that company everyone had heard about. And yet it was. Over 70 years of deception and empty promises have created a reputation of distrust. We earned it. And it is left to us to change it.

I have also seen that, for those people who "figure it out," their lives are forever enriched financially, physically, emotionally, and spiritually by the journey of Network Marketing. Some would say that it's not fair that only a few people create the success they want in Network Marketing. I would say that everyone who "takes a look" at Network Marketing as a part-time income or a significant wealth-building alternative has the same opportunity to succeed. Life is not fair if you define fairness as "everyone wins." My mentors never promised me life would be fair. They just promised me it would "be." The rest was up to me.

In 2012, had I stuck it out, I would have been retiring from Foster Farms. That's not a bad thing, just different. I loved the people there and even enjoyed the work.

Instead, I have traveled to every state in our union at least twice, to every province and territory of Canada, and to over 20 fascinating countries (including my favorite, Cuba, three times). I've built incredible relationships with thousands of people from all over the world and had incredible successes, as well as my share of mind-bending failures. My favorite people in the world are still my high school buddies, and my favorite places in the world are still where I call home—beautiful Coeur d'Alene, Idaho, and Lanai, Hawaii. I am grateful to be able to clearly make the distinction between my life as it is and what it would have been had I stayed at Foster Farms.

I suppose a person can figure out how something won't work or figure out how it will. Either way, each attitude is a self-fulfilling prophecy.

Success

In March 1992, *SUCCESS* magazine featured the Network Marketing industry's skyrocketing success as its lead story. It was the first time a mainstream publication had done so in the industry's 50-year history. That is your favorite chicken chopper turned CEO, Richard Bliss Brooke, in the middle picture. (You can read about how they selected him in *Mach2: The Art of Vision & Self-Motivation*.) It outsold every issue in the 100-year history of the magazine.

Richard Bliss Brooke has been a full-time Network Marketing professional since 1977. He is a former member of the Board of Directors of the Direct Selling

Association, a senior member of the DSA Ethics Committee, as well as:

- Author of *The Four Year Career*® and *Mach2: The Art of Vision & Self-Motivation*
- Owner of a Network Marketing company
- Industry Expert and Advocate
- Motivational Seminar Leader
- Ontological Coach

My own personal story is certainly exceptional and is not what the average person chooses to achieve or is capable of achieving in our business. Network Marketing is certainly not for everyone … perhaps not even for most people. And those who do choose to pursue it usually lose interest in the income opportunity. Building a sales organization takes time, usually years, and most people do not stick with it.

Fortunately, when the products are excellent, even those people who give up on the income opportunity may choose to keep using the products and recommending them when it is convenient. These are the people who make up most of the "sales force."

CONTENTS

FOREWORD

"It is in the nature of revolution, the overturning of an existing order, that at its inception a very small number of people are involved. The process in fact, begins with one person and an idea, an idea that persuades a second, then a third and a fourth, and gathers force until the idea is successfully contradicted, absorbed into conventional wisdom, or actually turns the world upside down. A revolution requires not only ammunition, but also weapons and men willing to use them and willing to be slain in the battle. In an intellectual revolution, there must be ideas and advocates willing to challenge an entire profession, the establishment itself, willing to spend their reputations and careers in spreading the idea through deeds as well as words."

JUDE WANNISKI, 1936-2005
The Way the World Works (Touchstone Books, 1978)

"When Galileo invited scholars to look through his telescope in order to see the new evidence, they flatly refused. They didn't want to see any data that might count against the earth-centric view of the universe. It is difficult to think of a more revelatory episode of cognitive dissonance. They simply shut their eyes."

MATTHEW SYED
Black Box Thinking: Why Most People Never Learn from Their Mistakes--But Some Do (Portfolio, 2015)

This book is intended to be a fair and honest view of the Network Marketing income model. The core profession has been historically called Direct Sales, where a person directly sells a product or service to others outside of a retail establishment. Direct Sales has been a profession for thousands of years. In fact, it is the original method of sales and business.

In 1945, **California Vitamins** revolutionized the direct sales industry when they allowed all sales reps to recruit other sales reps and earn a commission on their sales ... and the sales of many generations of sales reps below them. This created a compounding, or geometric progression, possibility of the growth of the sales force because every customer could become a sales rep and begin building a sales team. The classic 4 who recruit 4 who recruit 4 $(1 - 4 - 16 - 64)$ presentation was born to show people how a sales organization could grow.

The marketplace was drawn to Network Marketing because the business model allowed for a person to build a sales team of dozens, maybe hundreds, maybe even thousands of people by only enrolling a few themselves. This leverage of time and effort allowed people to see a wealth-building opportunity.

Building a sales team is a lot harder than it looks on paper. Fewer than 10% who attempt to build any size team actually do so, and the percentage of people who build one into the hundreds is single digits. The percentage of people who build one into the thousands is far less than 1%.

Although the odds of building any kind of wealth are slim, that does not deter people from going for it. Why not? There is little to lose as long as you are smart with your money … and a great deal to gain. And in the end, most people (90%) who join any company just do so because they love the products and the people, and they are very happy earning a few hundred dollars or less each month by merely recommending the products to others.

Network Marketing is also referred to as Multi-level Marketing, Relationship Marketing, or Social Marketing. It is present in many messages and exists in many sales channels, including the Internet and even retail establishments. Occasionally, the classic pyramid scheme masquerades as a Network Marketing company. The differences are clear and easy to discern, and the guidelines are detailed in chapter 2.

The Network Marketing profession produces now over $34 billion in annual sales by 18 million US-based direct sellers and is represented by The Direct Selling Association, a 100-plus-year-old trade association based in Washington, D.C.

There are several levels of participation for those choosing to get involved in Network Marketing.

Customers

A customer is created when an existing customer (who could also be a distributor) recommends a product they love, and the new customer tries and likes the product at the price charged. Customers may order randomly as needed or set themselves up on auto ship.

Distributors

This level is designed for customers who want to recommend the product and are OK with earning a small profit from each sale. Distributors usually do not have to inventory product, but rather, just refer the new customer to the website and the company pays the distributor the profits from the sale. Inventorying product is of course preferable, as some customers want to take delivery immediately. Being a distributor is relatively easy and does not require a lot of time or lifestyle changes. Whether a distributor "succeeds" and remains a distributor depends generally on whether they create and maintain any customers.

90% of all Network Marketing participants are either customers or distributors in most companies.

Sales Leaders
Sales Leaders have the intention of building a sales team of distributors and other Sales Leaders. The Four Year Career was written about, and for, Sales Leaders: ambitious and courageous people who are committed to creating financial freedom.

POSSIBILITIES

My personal story, other stories, and examples of "possibilities" shared herein are absolutely the exceptions rather than the average results. The "average" person who joins any Network Marketing company usually does not manage his or her motivation adequately and ends up quitting before earning a sustained profit. In fact, most people do. This book is not about claiming what will happen for you, but rather giving you enough information to decide for yourself what might be possible.

Our profession is often criticized and censored for telling our stories and showing what is possible. The reason is, historically, possibilities have been represented as promises. Success in Network Marketing requires the same types of talents, efforts, and commitments required to succeed in any business. There is no free lunch here ... because freedom is not free.

CHAPTER ONE

A Four Year Career vs. A Forty Year Career?

Security is mostly a superstition. It does not exist in nature, nor do the children of men as a whole experience it. Avoiding danger is no safer in the long run than outright exposure. Life is either a daring adventure, or nothing.

– HELEN KELLER

Since the dawn of the Industrial Revolution, over 250 years ago, the idea of a career has been to work (at least) 40 hours a week for 40 years for 40% of what was never enough for the first 40 years.

The 40/40/40 Plan

The mandated path for most of us was:

1. Get a good education … a four year degree is your ticket.
2. Get a good job with a big company … with lots of benefits.
3. Work for 40 years to retire and enjoy the golden years.

Things have changed a lot since then. Your company is more likely to file bankruptcy to avoid paying your retirement than it is to honor it. Even states, counties, and cities are starting to face the fact that they overpromised and can't deliver, and are filing bankruptcy to ditch their retirement and health care obligations. And even if the retirement is there … even a 401k, there is rarely enough income from this model to have a grand ol' time in your golden years. Most people just hunker down and run out the clock. I don't know, maybe they think this is a trial run and they get another shot at it.

Investing in Your Future

Today, tech companies are paying kids (16-20 year olds) to pass on college and "get in here and create products with us *now*."

Also, most young adults following the college model do end up well trained to get a job, but are also well saddled with debt. This debt cannot be discharged in bankruptcy, it can rarely be renegotiated, and most people are ill-afforded to pay it off. Since most people in their 30s and 40s are not even working in the careers they majored in, the debt they are carrying is a depressing load.

If you are intent on becoming a doctor, lawyer, engineer, or CPA, the more education you get, the better. There are additional viable options if you choose to consider them. The cheese has been moved.[1]

Not only has the cheese moved, it has been cut up in a lot of different pieces and put in different places. There is a big piece of it over in Network Marketing.

The Four Year Career Option

The Four Year Career was originally conceived in 1977. Although I never went to college, I was working with a few college kids on building their Network Marketing businesses. I was living in Des Moines, Iowa, so I decided to interview some marketing students at Drake University to understand the effort and cost they were investing for four years of college in relationship to the outcome.

What I was thinking about was how successful someone COULD be if they invested some of their effort and studying hours into building a network. I knew if someone invested even a fraction of the capital (in training, travel, tools, marketing, etc.) and a fraction of the time, that instead of graduating with debt and begging for a job, they could graduate with a $5,000 a month residual income. What kind of job would they end up accepting, what kind of posture would they have in looking for a job, where would they choose to live if they graduated with Freedom? I expect their choices and the story of their lives would be a lot different.

---

[1] *Who Moved My Cheese?* by Spencer Johnson

Ultimately, I found that college kids were not the best candidates for this kind of career … too many distractions. So, The Four Year Career became a business plan for people who were ready for a change in their lifestyles, financial security, and professional development.

The "four years" is arbitrary. There is no magic number of years. I have seen people get free in less than a year's worth of effort while others take 6-7 years. And, of course, most people never follow the plan and end up right back in their old lives. That is not a bad thing. We all have it pretty good regardless of our chosen career path.

The Investment Strategy

What about investment strategies? The models for us to choose from have traditionally been real estate and equities.

Liquid Investments/Equities

Most of us already have these kinds of investments to some extent. We take what we can or will out of our paychecks, after paying taxes and all of our bills. If we are fortunate and/or frugal, we might end up with 10% to invest … perhaps $500 to $1,000 a month. For many people, it's just the opposite … they are going in debt $500 to $1,000 a month and are just "hoping" something will change. Which group are you? Who do you know in the latter group? What are their options for change?

The save and invest system does work when we work it. We need to invest consistently, every month, and we need to invest in ways that produce at least an aggressive return over time, such as 7%. Any one of us who started doing this from our first working years would end up with a sizable nest egg. For those who waited, the results are less favorable. And equities can go from 100% to zero overnight if you pick the wrong investment, such as Enron, Global Crossing, MCI, AIG, Bear Stearns, Washington Mutual, IndyMac, Goldman Sachs, Kodak, Hostess, General Motors, Saab, American Airlines, MF Global, Borders, Solyndra, Lehman Brothers, Delta Airlines, WorldCom, etc.

Take a close look at the compounding chart for a reality check. Invest $500 a month at 7% from age 30 to 70, and you will have over $1.3 million. That asset will pay you $84,000 a year for life at 7%. How much would you need to invest to end up with the same amount if you wait until you are 50?

In order to achieve the same cash value in only 20 years (starting at age 50 through age 70), your required monthly investment is nearly $2,500! And notice I used a 7% return. That is quite a generous assumption. What are you earning on your investments on average since you started investing? 2%, 7%, or 10%?

Total cash value of saving $500/month compounded* at 7% for 40 years: **$1,320,062**

Total cash value of saving $500/month compounded* at 7% for 20 years: **$261,983**

The difference is **$1,058,079** * Compounded Monthly

Real Estate

Many of us gain most of our net worth through the payments we make over time on our own homes. This works because we must pay someone for a place to live; therefore, we are consistent with the investment. In higher-end markets and any waterfront communities, historically the return is much more than 7%. However, we have also seen market corrections that have dropped real estate values by up to 50%, even in those coveted California and Florida markets.

The Challenge

For most people who consider these strategies, it is deciding what to invest in, and more importantly, where to get the money to invest. These strategies work great if you have the extra $1,000 a month to invest every month without fail for 25 years.

And unfortunately, the downturns in the markets rarely give notice. Those who even invest for a living are, for the most part, completely caught off guard. Those of us who invest as a necessity are caught in the landslide.

CHAPTER TWO

WHY NETWORK MARKETING?

Far better it is to dare mighty things, to win glorious triumphs, even though checkered by failure, than to take rank with those poor spirits who neither enjoy much nor suffer much, because they live in the gray twilight that knows neither victory nor defeat.

– THEODORE ROOSEVELT

There is a third strategy that anyone can employ to build extraordinary wealth and financial freedom, regardless of age, experience, education, income level, or social status: Asset Income from Network Marketing.

A Network Marketing Income Offers Huge Advantages

1. You can build it part-time, any time.
2. You can build it from anywhere, any city, any virtual office.
3. You can launch it for $500 to $1,000.
4. You are in business for yourself, but not *by* yourself, meaning your host company will do all the heavy investing and lifting— from product development, legal groundwork, customer service, data processing, banking, sales training, marketing, branding, and even social media.
5. Your business partners—those above you in the network in terms of seniority and lineage—have a vested interest in your success. Somewhere in your team, someone is making it work, and they want more than anything to teach and motivate you to make it work.
6. You can create enough tax deductions alone each year to make it worthwhile.
7. You can learn it while you earn it. You can create cash flow your first month.
8. You can earn an extra $500, $1,000, $5,000 or more a month— every month—to invest in the traditional options of real estate and equities.
9. With time and success, your income will be produced for you by hundreds, perhaps even thousands of people, each pursuing their own success. This creates an Asset Income, meaning it could go on forever regardless of whether you are working hard at it or not. A pure Asset Income creates an asset … or net worth.

The asset value of your Network Marketing income will be approximately 200 times your monthly income. If you are earning $5,000 a month in residual Asset Income, and you can rely on it continuing, your Asset Income could be worth $1 million.

How much would you have to earn to invest enough to build $1 million in real estate or equities? How long would it take? How much would you have to sacrifice in your *lifestyle* to do it?

It is 200 times easier to build your net worth all three ways, using your Network Marketing income to fund the other two options. And you can get to your target net worth in five to ten years versus it taking your whole lifetime.

Yeah, But Why Network Marketing? Let's Start With a Couple of Simple Facts

Fact #1: It's legal.

In the US and around the world in over 70 countries, Network Marketing has been legally used for product distribution and compensating Distributors for more than 70 years.

During this time, Network Marketing has repeatedly been upheld by the federal and state courts as a legal distribution and compensation method when the following legal guidelines are followed:

1. The main objective of the business is selling viable products or

services at a market-driven price. Meaning, there is a market for the product from consumers absent of the financial opportunity. The test is simple. Would you or do you have customers who are buying this product without any connection to the Network Marketing financial opportunity? Is it a real product at a market-driven price or is the product a shill in a money game?

2. Potential incomes can't be promised. Even hypothetical incomes can't be inferred without the appropriate disclaimers. This is not an even playing field with the rest of the business world; even lotteries get to hype us into thinking we might win millions (even though we have better odds of getting struck by lightning). Beware of Network Marketing companies that hype the income without transparency.

3. Distributors are not paid for the act of recruiting others (headhunting fees). Income has to come entirely from the sale of products.

There are many products or services that Distributors will be "customers" for as long as there is a financial opportunity to go with it. The means justify the end. Unfortunately, when all the shine wears off, no one continues to use the product. This is a pyramid scheme. The true test of a legitimate Network Marketing company is whether most of the product is sold to consumers who are not earning any commissions or royalties from the opportunity. Most Network Marketing Distributors start out pursuing the income opportunity, but once they give up, they settle in to being customers. Most companies' total sales are made up of these "wholesale" customers. Maybe they sell enough to get theirs for free. This is easily 70% of most Network Marketing sales forces. They don't have any sales reps on their teams. They are just using the product. They are customers. The other 30% is made up of those earning a few hundred to a few thousand dollars a month.

A key question to ask if you are concerned is, "What percent of total company sales goes to people who are not also earning a royalty check on their sales organization?" This is the true definition of a customer: someone buying the product and the only motive is to buy the product. If at least 50% or so of sales are going to customers, it is likely a legitimate business.

The concept attracts very dynamic promoters—some are ethical, some are not. Many Network Marketing companies have crossed the line legally and have been the subject of negative media, as well as civil and criminal penalties. However, I've also read in the last few years about the banking and investment industries, the oil industry, and the drug industry being indicted, prosecuted, fined, and sometimes seeing their executives imprisoned. Such is the nature of free enterprise in the wild, wild West.

Fact #2: Most companies fail, some succeed.

There are an estimated 1,000 Network Marketing firms distributing over $36 billion a year in goods and services in the US alone. *About 200* of those are Direct Selling Association (DSA) members. *There are a few legitimate and successful companies that are **not** DSA members* for reasons of their own. DSA membership is a high bar of legal and ethical scrutiny. A DSA member company has already been vetted by a rigorous process. This does not mean that just because a company is a DSA member that it is totally legitimate. You need to do your own analysis.

Most Network Marketing companies do not succeed. Most restaurants do not. Most dry cleaners do not. Most companies we went to work for just out of college or high school have already failed.

And some do succeed. Herbalife, Mary Kay, Forever Living Products, Nu Skin, and USANA are multi-billion dollar brands and have been in business and growing steadily for 30 to 60 years. Hundreds of other companies sell between $10 million and $1 billion a year through millions of independent brand representatives.

This is the nature of free markets and enterprise.

Fact #3: Most Distributors give up long before they could have succeeded.

Some rare individual Distributors have earned and enjoyed long-standing Asset Royalty Income fortunes of *$1 million or more* per year, for years. Some elite business builders, after investing 5 to 10 years, earn $25,000 to $100,000 a month. Many more earn from $1,000 to $10,000 a month. And the masses earn a few hundred.

And all of the above are those who did not quit.

Most individuals who pursue building a Network Marketing business give up before they see the level of success for which they hoped.

The average Network Marketer never creates enough success to warrant doing anything beyond buying product at wholesale. The fact is, people with average ambition, commitment, and effort usually don't do well in a business like Network Marketing.

Is that the fault of the system or the individual? Both, I think.

Network Marketing is not easy. Who do you know that is right now looking to get involved in Network Marketing? No one, unless they are already involved.

90% of new realtors never sell a house and end up quitting. The world is made up of those who want to achieve and those who do. The percentages are about 90/10. Network Marketing does not magically change that.

We have a long way to go in educating the public and treating the public with respect and honor before there will be a public demand for our profession. That is one of the intentions of this book.

To be successful, one must have a high level of personal confidence, love talking to people, be comfortable creating new relationships every day, be coachable, and most importantly, be a proud ambassador of the Network Marketing profession.

Fact #4: <u>We</u> are a major player in the global economy, and we are growing!

The Network Marketing method of marketing as an industry has grown 18 out of the last 20 years, including over 90% in just the past 10 years. A staggering *$183 billion* worth of goods and services are sold worldwide each year in this industry. There are 20 million Americans and 99 million people worldwide who participate at some level in this concept.

Twenty-five years ago there were no books written on the subject of Network Marketing. Now there are dozens … some have sold millions

The Top 12 Billion Dollar Network Marketing Companies: 2015 Revenue

$9.5 billion

$6.16 billion

$4.47 billion

VORWERK

$4 billion

 INFINITUS

$3.88 billion

MARY KAY®

$3.7 billion

 PERFECT

$3.58 billion

 natura

$2.41 billion

 Tupperware®

$2.28 billion

 NU SKIN. THE DIFFERENCE. DEMONSTRATED.™

$2.25 billion

 TIENS

$1.55 billion

PRIMERICA

$1.41 billion

of copies. Fifteen years ago no mainstream magazines, newspapers, or television shows had featured the positive, uplifting opportunity of Network Marketing. Now there are hundreds of examples. Ten years ago there were virtually no "thought leaders" who endorsed our profession. Now many of them do.

There are thousands of companies and millions of sales representatives: all looking to build their teams. This idea's time has come. And it is about to explode … in a good way.

It Works

The bottom line is, Network Marketing works and has worked to build extra—to extraordinary—individual wealth for more than 60 years. Some of the smartest people in the world are taking advantage of it.

Tony Robbins, American motivational speaker and author of *Unlimited Power, Unleash the Power Within* and *Awaken the Giant Within*

> "What's beautiful about Network Marketing is you get all the benefits of being a business owner, without all the headaches, and without the same level of risk. And so I think Network Marketing's amazing!"

Richard Branson, Founder of Virgin Group, business magnate, investor, and philanthropist

> "I'm a tremendous Believer in Network Marketing."

Jim Rohn, entrepreneur, author and motivational speaker

> "Network Marketing is really the greatest source of grassroots capitalism, because it teaches people how to take a small bit of capital, that is our time, and build the American dream."

Bob Proctor, the "Foremost Personal Achievement Philosopher"

> "What you sow, you reap. It's the law of nature. Network Marketing is perfectly aligned with that. You truly get EXACTLY what you are worth. NO nepotism, NO favoritism. That's rare today."

Brian Tracy, business coach, bestselling author, thought leader

> "The future of Network Marketing is unlimited. There's no end in sight. It will continue to grow, because better people are getting into it. It will be one of the respected business methods in the world."

Darren Hardy, Publisher of *SUCCESS* Magazine

> "The future of employment is self-employment. Direct selling is one of the few business opportunities that offers average people, with above average ambition, to achieve an above average lifestyle, peace of mind, and financial security."

Robert T. Kiyosaki, author of *Rich Dad Poor Dad* and *The Business of the 21st Century*

> "… Direct Selling gives people the opportunity, with very low risk and very low financial commitment, to build their own income—generating assets and acquiring great wealth."

Stephen Covey, author of *The Seven Habits of Highly Effective People*

> "Network Marketing has come of age. It's undeniable that it has become a way to entrepreneurship and independence for millions of people."

David Bach, author of the *New York Times* bestseller *The Automatic Millionaire*

> "… you don't need to create a business plan or create a product. You only need to find a reputable company, one that you trust, that offers a product or service you believe in and can get passionate about."

Tom Peters, legendary management expert and author of *In Search of Excellence* and *The Circle of Innovation*

> "… the first truly revolutionary shift in marketing since the advent of 'modern' marketing at P&G and the Harvard Business School 50 to 75 years ago."

Jim Collins, author of *Built to Last* and *Good to Great*

"… how the best organizations of the future might run – in the spirit of partnership and freedom, not ownership and control."

Ray Chambers, entrepreneur, philanthropist, humanitarian, and owner of Princess House

"The Direct Selling business model is one that can level the playing field and close the gap between the haves and have-nots."

Roger Barnett, New York investment banker, multi-billionaire, and owner of Shaklee

"… best-kept secret of the business world."

Dave Ramsey, *New York Times* bestselling author and radio host

"Multi-level Marketing, Network Marketing, and Direct Sales are the names used by those in that type of company to describe how their business models work. Their detractors call what they do 'one of those pyramid schemes' with a snarl. These companies are not pyramid schemes; they are a legitimate method for some people to make some side money and sometimes to literally build their own business."

Warren Buffett, billionaire investor and owner of three Direct Selling/Network Marketing companies

"The best investment Berkshire Hathaway ever made."

CHAPTER THREE

NETWORK MARKETING MYTHS

Every man takes the limits of his own field
of vision for the limits of the world.

– ARTHUR SCHOPENHAUER

Myth #1: Getting in on the ground floor is the best path to success in a Network Marketing company.

The truth is, it is the worst time to join. Most companies, including Network Marketing companies, go out of business in their first five years. Of course, no company is going to tell you that in their promotional materials. Everyone involved at the start of any company hopes it will succeed.

Another risk with a new company is that no company has its best foot forward early on. It takes years to develop competent, experienced staff, reliable procedures, and efficient services.

The best time to join a Network Marketing company is when it is at least five years old, or backed by a larger company. By then, it has demonstrated a commitment and ability to:

- Grow ethically
- Stay in business
- Honor its Distributors and Customers

And yet, this allows you the opportunity to get involved with the company before they are so well-known that everyone has either already given them a try, or decided they aren't interested.

Now, of course, if everyone adhered to this sage advice, none of us would be here. To the pioneers and courageous (the risk-takers) come both the thrill of victory and the agony of defeat. The ground floor is not for the faint of heart.

Myth #2: Network Marketing is an opportunity for someone who is not doing well financially to make some money—maybe even a lot of money.

Unfortunately, many of the success stories have perpetuated this myth with a rags-to-riches theme. Although there are enough people to substantiate the myth, it is still a myth.

The same skills it takes to succeed in any marketing business are required in Network Marketing:

- You must be assertive
- You must have confidence
- You must be dynamic in your ability to express yourself
- You must have enough resources to propel yourself through the challenges

Your resources should include working capital, contacts, time, discipline, and a positive, crystal-clear vision of where you intend to go with your business—whether it is easy or not.

The truth is that many people who are struggling financially are doing so for a number of reasons, including low self-esteem and/or lack of the basic skills and preparation that allow one to succeed in anything. Network Marketing is a powerful and dynamic economic model, but not so powerful that it can overcome a person's lack of readiness or persistence.

The fact is that the people who are already successful in whatever they do, tend to also succeed in Network Marketing. The great part is, they are apt to do better financially in Network Marketing because the economic dynamics are so powerful. Successful people are rarely in a profession where they can earn on the leverage of thousands of other people. Real estate agents, teachers, coaches, medical professionals, counselors, small business owners, beauty professionals, and physical fitness professionals may be stellar performers in their domains, but how do they create the opportunity to earn on the efforts of thousands of others in their same profession? Here, they can.

Myth #3: Network Marketers succeed by being in the right place at the right time.

Network Marketing is a business; it is not a hobby, a game, a scheme, a deal, or something in which to dabble. People who treat it lightly do not succeed. People who treat it as a new career, a profession, and a business have a reasonable opportunity to make it pay off very well. Most people invite a few people to look and then quit. Those who master it invite a few people every day for a year or two, and in that "practice," they hone the art of listening more than talking, interpret rejection in a learning way, and discover how to craft their offers in such a way that someone actually WANTS to hear more. Just like any worthwhile career, it takes time, patience, and repetition.

Myth #4: The way Network Marketing works is the "big guys" make all their money off the "little guys."

The "big guys, little guys" myth is usually perpetuated by people who define fairness as "everyone gets the same benefits, regardless of their contributions." That is how socialism works, not how Network Marketing works.

In Network Marketing, the people who attract, train, and motivate the most salespeople earn the most money. Period.

There are basically three levels of participation:

Customers

This is someone who gets involved just to use the products and buy them at the lowest cost. This often requires a little higher minimum order and an annual renewal fee, very much like being a member of Costco. Many Distributors end up just being customers after pursuing the income opportunity and deciding it is not for them.

Distributors

A Distributor focuses their efforts on just selling the products. In many cases, they do not understand the income opportunity well enough to sell it.

A Distributor will earn 20% to 50% commission on their own personal sales, and the upper limit of their income will usually be in the hundreds of dollars a month.

Sales Leaders

A Sales Leader is someone who is a customer, a retailer, and an inviter. They understand the business model well enough to know the best upside is in getting Geometric Progression to work for them. Therefore, they are always inviting others to "just take a look" at the opportunity.

A Sales Leader may enroll as many as 100 people to build with them. Out of those, most will just use the product, some will retail it, and a few will actually do what the Sales Leader did by enrolling others.

To be a successful Sales Leader, one must be able to enroll lots of people to sell with them, and they must be able to train and motivate the group to continue growing. The better one is in these roles, the more money one will earn.

In simple terms, if a person sells a little and enrolls just a few people, they will earn far less than someone who sells a lot and enrolls, motivates, and trains a group that grows. That's basic capitalism, which most North Americans consider quite fair.

Myth #5: You have to use your friends and family to make any money in Network Marketing.

The truth is, you do not and you should not. Your friends and family should only become a part of your business if it serves them to do so. If it serves them—if they see an opportunity for themselves just like you did—then they are not being used; they are being served. If you do not believe your opportunity can serve them, do not offer it to them.

An opportunity that truly inspires *you* will most likely inspire them as well. Offer it to them. If they say no, respect and honor their viewpoint and do not make a nuisance of yourself.

Myth #6: If Network Marketing really worked, everyone would get involved and the market would be saturated.

The truth is, although this is mathematically possible, history has proven that saturation is not an issue. There are many companies you will see featured in this book that have been in business for 30 to 50 years doing billions of dollars a year in business with millions of sales reps. Yet you are not one of them. Nor are 298 million people in the US and 6.9 billion people worldwide.

Plus, you might consider a great leader who personally sponsored 12 people 2,000 years ago. They have all been recruiting via weekly opportunity meetings and one-on-ones for all of those 2,000 years. And yet most of the world does not subscribe to their program.

CHAPTER FOUR

TRADITIONAL SALES VS. NETWORK MARKETING

Many people fear nothing more terribly than to take a position which stands out sharply and clearly from the prevailing opinion. The tendency of most is to adopt a view that is so ambiguous that it will include everything and so popular that it will include everybody …

– MARTIN LUTHER KING, JR.

Most of us grew up with a traditional selling paradigm. It sounds like this … if you have the opportunity to earn money with a product, what you are supposed to do is sell a lot of product. The more you sell, the more money you earn. Right?

In the traditional selling paradigm, if you had a goal of selling $1 million worth of product a month, you might hire 100 full-time, professional salespeople to work for you, giving them each a territory and a quota of $10,000 in sales per month. If they couldn't meet that quota, you would fire them and find other salespeople who could. And you would keep hiring and firing (forever) seeking to find the 100 who would consistently meet your quota. (And if you didn't own the company, the owners would fire you if you didn't.)

While Network Marketing is a form of selling, there are some very important distinctions. As a Network Marketer, you would use a very different *paradigm* to achieve the same $1 million in sales.

Instead of full-time, professional salespeople with terrifying quotas, Network Marketing is based on satisfied customers, most of whom do not like to sell, but are happy to tell others about the products they use themselves. These customers are not full-time or part-time employees. They are some-time, independent volunteers with no quotas and no protected territories. They "work" *when they feel like it*.

Network Marketing is not about personally selling a lot of product, although some Distributors do. It is about **using** and **recommending** the product and, IF you see and believe in the wealth-building model of Geometric Progression, finding a lot of others to do the same.

Network Marketing is simply a lot of people "selling" a little bit *each*.

The differences between **salespeople** and **Network Marketing people** are:

SALES		NETWORK MARKETING
Full-time	**vs.**	Some-time
Salespeople	**vs.**	Customers
Employees	**vs.**	Volunteers
Quotas	**vs.**	Incentives
Protected Territories	**vs.**	No Territories

To Sell $1,000,000:

100 salespeople each sell $10,000 = $1,000,000	**vs.**	10,000 volunteers each sell $100 = $1,000,000

CHAPTER FIVE

HOW IT WORKS

Nothing worthwhile really ever comes easily. Work, continuous work and hard work, is the only way you will accomplish results that last. Whatever you want in life, you must give up something to get it. The greater the value, the greater the sacrifice required of you.

There's a price to pay if you want to make things better, a price to pay for just leaving things as they are. The highway to success is a toll road. Everything has a price.

– UNKNOWN

There are Three Basic Activities Required to Create Your Own Four Year Career

1. Be a Customer

First, become your own best customer. USE all of your company's products in as many ways as possible to discover your favorites. Create your own best product story. You will want to be able to tell people exactly what this product did for you that made you want to use it forever and share it with others. The more powerful your own story, the more impact you will have in recommending the product to others—and most importantly, you won't be "selling" it, you will just be recommending it.

2. Recommend

This is where most people think they have to sell the product. It's better to see yourself just recommending it, like you would a good movie or restaurant. You listen to the people around you … listen to their problems. And when someone shares a problem your product can solve, just tell them your story. Let them decide if it is right for them. If you recommend a great Italian place and the person says, "I don't like Italian," then the conversation is probably over. If they say, "That place is too expensive," you just let it go as their opinion. You don't argue, right? Don't sell or argue with customers either. Just recommend it. If it is a fit, perfect. If not, let it go. This is how successful Network Marketers establish lots of customers over time and move lots of product without making a nuisance of themselves.

3. Invite to "Just Take a Look"

Inviting people is like recommending the product, only you are inviting them to "just take a look" at the income opportunity. The best way to do this is with a tool like a CD, DVD, brochure, website, or app. Those who master inviting eventually master The Four Year Career.

Again, this is not selling, convincing, or arguing. People are either ready in their lives right now to look at new options, or they are not. Arguing with them about whether they have the time or money to get started, or whether they are good at selling is a waste of time and energy. (Although it is fun to "let" someone "sell" you on why they can't sell.)

You may not have as great an income story to tell your prospects as you do a product story. That is what your "upline" partners are for. Tell their stories. Here are just a couple keys to being an effective inviter:

1. Be convinced yourself … in your product, your company, and The Four Year Career. Your conviction should show up as enthusiasm, confidence, peace, patience, acceptance, love, and leadership.
2. Be interesting. Not by what you say, what you drive, or how you hype, but by being *interested* … interested in them. Ask curiosity questions and **LISTEN**. You will be amazed at how interesting people are … their lives, their families, their careers, their heartaches, and their dreams. In this process they will either tell you exactly what is missing in their lives that your invite may help solve … or they won't. Invite those who reveal their own opportunities.

CHAPTER SIX

FOUR CORNERSTONES OF THE FOUR YEAR CAREER

The American Pioneers HAD to become successful entrepreneurs …
the Native Americans wouldn't hire them.

– RICHARD BLISS BROOKE

Below is a model of The Four Year Career. Each person represented is a Sales Leader, meaning they are doing all three activities in the last chapter.

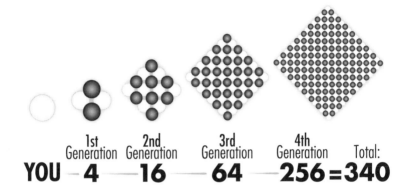

YOU — **4** — **16** — **64** — **256** = **340**

1st Generation — 2nd Generation — 3rd Generation — 4th Generation — Total:

**You enroll 4 (who each enroll 4)
for 16 (who each enroll 4)
for 64 (who each enroll 4) for 256**

Each of you uses and recommends just an average of $100 a month in products for $34,000 in monthly sales, earning an average of 10% on each generation of sales for an Asset Income of $3,410 a month.

The Four Cornerstones:

**1. The People
2. Product Sales
3. Your Asset Income
4. The Asset Value**

Geometric progression of your sales team's growth is easy to show on paper as a hypothetical but takes leadership, motivation, and dedicated effort for years to accomplish. Most people (an understatement) do not maintain their motivation to continue.

The First Cornerstone is the People

Network Marketing is a lot of people selling a little bit each. Remember the example of traditional sales where the goal was to sell $1 million a month in products? Hire 100 superstars and give them a $10,000 a month quota. 100 times $10,000 is $1 million. In Network Marketing, you swap the numbers: 10,000 "anybody" volunteers using and selling a little bit each.

So the question is how do we get 10,000 people … or even 1,000?

Two laws allow us to gather 1,000 people. The first was written by the creators for the Network Marketing concept who said, in essence: "Anyone can, and should sponsor others." This allows the second law: Geometric Progression.

This is How the Rich Get Richer and the Poor Get Poorer

If you had $1 million today to invest at 10%:

- In 7 years, you would have $2 million
- In 14 years, you would have $4 million
- In 21 years, you would have $8 million

With $8 million at 10% you would be earning $800,000 a year in interest alone. Eventually, whether it is at $800,000 a year or $2 million a year, you tire of spending it (on assets that do not appreciate).

In many "old money" families, this investment compounding has gone on for so many generations, they can't possibly spend all the interest-income produced. They are on autopilot to just keep getting richer.

- *Geometric Progression is to Network Marketing what compounding is to wealth building.*
- The question is: how do you get 1,000 people to be "recommending for you"?
- The answer is: you don't. You just get a few … like four, and lead them to do the same.

The path to gathering 1,000, 2,000, or 30,000 people to "sell for you" in Network Marketing is Geometric Progression. This is made possible by the Rule of Law in Network Marketing … that everyone, regardless of rank or time involved, is encouraged to invite and enroll others. If you have been involved for one day you are encouraged to invite and enroll others. This is the same if you have been involved for 10 years and are earning $10,000 a month. Everyone enrolls new sales representatives. This creates the compounding impact.

You enroll four who each enroll four who each enroll four, etc. 1 – 4 – 16 – 64 – 256 – 1,024 and so on.

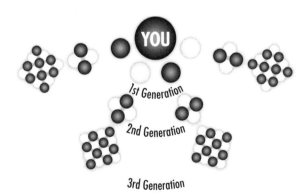

No Network Marketer's organization looks exactly like this one. This is merely an illustration of a mathematical formula that shows the dynamic and potential available. There is no way to control how many, or how few, people any one Distributor will sponsor.

Geometric progression of your sales team's growth is easy to show on paper as a hypothetical but takes leadership, motivation, and dedicated effort for years to accomplish. Most people (an understatement) do not maintain their motivation to continue.

It's Not Nearly as Easy as It Appears on Paper

This progression can quickly be overwhelming. But your role in Network Marketing is just to get the first four—not the whole bunch. Focus your attention on just the first four. And in actuality, you may build in units of two or three depending on your particular compensation model … the same concept holds true.

The key to understanding the geometric opportunity lies in a simple question:

> *"If you really, really wanted to,* could you find four people, anywhere in North America, to do this?" Before you answer, let's define "do this."

"Doing this" … being a Sales Leader is:

1. Using the products
2. Recommending the products to others in need/want
3. Inviting others to "just take a look"

So I ask you again. If you really, really wanted to, could you find four people in the next four to six months?

Now, if you are not sure, what if I told you I would give you $5,000 for each of them … $20,000 cash if you get four in the next four months? Then could you? Would you?

Most people would answer yes. The reason is, if they really "wanted to," anything like this is doable. Getting four people to earn more income is not THAT hard to do.

If you answered YES … lock in on that YES; it is the key to believing you can get 10,000. Why? Because if you believe you will get four … and they are four who are "doing it" … then they also will be facing the same question. Will they get four? If you are not sure … ask them. And what is usually the result of someone really, really wanting to do something—but more importantly—believing they will do it and being in action doing it? It eventually gets done.

Now remember, I am typing this on my laptop. Creating it in actual, real-life human production requires more than just simple keystrokes.

Perhaps you are "getting it" right now. Perhaps you need to let it rest or doodle it on a notepad … 1 – 2 – 4 – 8, 1 – 3 – 9 – 27, 1 – 4 – 16 – 64, 1 – 5 – 25 – 125.

This is how Geometric Progression will work for you. One person each believing they will get four creates … You – 4 – 16 – 64 – 256 – 1,024 – 4096 and so on.

The Second Cornerstone is Product Sales

Compared to the rest of the cornerstones, people are the most important and most challenging aspect to understand, believe in, and motivate. Product sales, however, are not. In a legitimate Network Marketing business, the brand representatives are very satisfied customers … with unbridled enthusiasm. They love the product. They love it so much they open their minds to becoming a Network Marketer and recommending it.

The average Network Marketer might only personally use and sell $100-$300 worth of product a month. There will always be

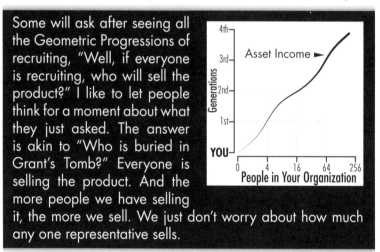

Some will ask after seeing all the Geometric Progressions of recruiting, "Well, if everyone is recruiting, who will sell the product?" I like to let people think for a moment about what they just asked. The answer is akin to "Who is buried in Grant's Tomb?" Everyone is selling the product. And the more people we have selling it, the more we sell. We just don't worry about how much any one representative sells.

exceptions. There are people who sell thousands a month. But as long as the product is compelling, the Distributors will sell it … or more accurately, recommend it. Sales are simply created by the Distributors using and offering products. So if you have 2,000 representatives each averaging $200 a month in consumption and sales, your business generates $400,000 a month in sales. Try personally selling $400,000 a month of any product. You would have to work about 1,000 hours a week. Your family would not like it.

The Third Cornerstone is Asset Income

This is the easiest cornerstone to understand and believe. Every Network Marketing company has a compensation plan that pays you on most, if not all, of the many generations of representatives in your group. This is the percent of sales volume you will earn on each generation of brand representatives.

Each company is very creative to incentivize (yes, this is now a word) certain business-building behaviors. The bottom line is that you can expect to earn between 5% and 10% on the sales of most of your organization, and even a small percent on all of it, providing you qualify to earn at the deepest generations. This gives you Asset Income. If your team's sales are $400,000 a month, you are earning between $20,000 and $40,000 a month. Basic math class.

The Fourth Cornerstone is The Asset Value

If you continue to use the theoretical model of four who sponsor four, etc., then at some point, perhaps around year two or three, 256 people would fill your fourth generation of Distributors. This would result in a total of 340 people in your Network Marketing organization.

If each of those Distributors uses and recommends just $200 of product per month, there would be 340 people selling a total of $68,000 worth of product monthly.

If you were paid an average royalty of 7% on that $68,000, your monthly check would be $4,760.

If you could count on it continuing long after you were done building it, then it is deemed residual and will have a corresponding asset value. $6,800 a month for example is worth about $1,200,000.

Examples of other income-producing assets would be real estate, dividend producing stocks, and patent and copyright royalties. All of these can be appraised for a value based on their income histories and future income prospects.

Think about it. What is your home worth? If you own it, what could you rent it for? If you are renting, you already know. If your home is worth $250,000 you might rent it for $1,500 a month for a 7% annual return on the investment.

Although you cannot sell a Distributorship for $1,200,000 that earns $6,800 a month (far too easy for one to build on their own), it is worth that to you as an asset.

So how do you know it will be residual?

The Answer … is in the Numbers

Look closely at the generations diagram that follows. Which

generation earns you the most income? Obviously, it is the fourth generation, which has four times as many people in it as the third generation before it. In fact, more than 75% of your group's sales volume—and therefore, over 75% of your earnings—are from your fourth generation Distributors.

In this scenario, however, we are showing your fourth generation Sales Leaders as just getting started in the business. As Sales Leaders

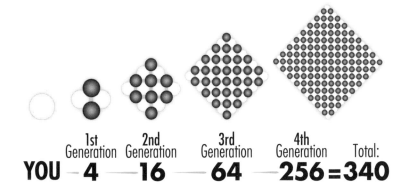

YOU — **4** — **16** — **64** — **256** = **340**

"doing it," they are inviting others to have a look, but they have not yet enrolled anyone themselves according to the diagram, as we do not show a fifth generation.

When each fourth generation Distributor gets their four, you would have added 1,024 new Distributors to your fifth generation. At $200 per Distributor in sales that translates into an additional $204,800 in sales.

Geometric progression of your sales team's growth is easy to show on paper as a hypothetical but takes leadership, motivation, and dedicated effort for years to accomplish. Most people (an understatement) do not maintain their motivation to continue.

THIS ONE PIECE OF THE PUZZLE PULLS IT ALL TOGETHER.

WHEN YOU UNDERSTAND THIS PIECE, YOU ARE LIKELY TO "GET IT" AND START TO UNDERSTAND THE POSSIBILITIES OF THE FOUR YEAR CAREER.

Everyone we have shown thus far in this hypothetical plan is what we call a Sales Leader. We have shown that each one gets four.

In order to get four to actually "do this" and be a Sales Leader, each Sales Leader will have to enroll many more than just four. Your first

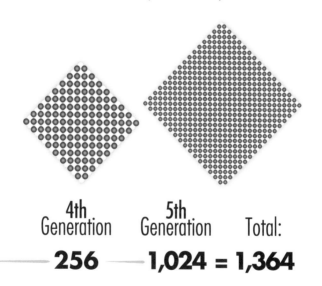

4th
Generation   5th
Generation   Total:
256 ——— 1,024 = 1,364

four are not likely going to be "the four." Each Sales Leader will likely enroll 20-100 people in order to get their own four Sales Leaders. The point is that in The Four Year Career, we only show Sales Leaders ... they are not the best of the best, just the best of the rest. They didn't quit. They are doing it.

So what happens to your Asset Income when they each get their own four? It grows by 400%. The definition of traditional Asset Income is that it grows slowly with no dramatic increase. However, when your Asset Income grows *geometrically*, it grows in significant increments.

So what about all the Non-Sales Leaders? What about the majority of new Distributors who did not end up "doing it"? Some quit and never continue even using the product. Some give up on the income opportunity, but remain loyal customers. Some sell a little, and some even enroll a few people here and there. But they are not Sales Leaders and NONE of them are shown in this plan. So what if you add them back in?

Adding them back in is more than a mind blowing exercise ... it is reality. Four years from now, if you build your Four Year Career, you will have more sales from customers and retailers as a total group than from Sales Leaders ... far more.

CHAPTER SEVEN

THE ASSET VALUE

If we don't change our direction we're likely to end up where we're headed.

– CHINESE PROVERB

Build your network right, and its sales and your income should flow long after you have anything to do with actively managing or growing it. This does not mean you ignore it or fail to nurture it. When we build or buy something that produces income without working it daily, it becomes an asset worth money in proportion to the income it produces.

In pursuing financial security or more from life, people tend to pursue real estate investments or stocks (which require money to invest). These investments require time to produce enough income to provide security. Imagine or calculate how long, and at what rate of investment, it would require to amass $1 million in rental real estate. It could easily take a lifetime of sacrifice, risk, and management. And $1 million in real estate might earn you $5,000 a month.

Compare that to investing $1,000 once and only 10-20 hours a week for four to five years to earn the same Asset Income with an asset

	1st Generation	2nd Generation	3rd Generation	4th Generation	Total:
YOU – 4	**– 16**	**– 64**	**– 256**	**= 340**	

$200 sales each x 340 people = $68,000

If each person has $200 in sales, that's 340 people earning total sales of $68,000. You could earn an average of 7%[*] on all of it per month:

$68,000 x 7%[*] = $4,760 a month = **$1,000,000 Asset Value**

$4,760 a month for example is worth about $1,000,000 at a 10% annualized return over the course of 10 years.

[*]Industry average.

value of $1,000,000. Which is more appealing and more achievable to you? Yeah, us too.

Now take it a step further and think about a powerful three-prong approach. You are building an Asset Income in Network Marketing while at the same time investing $1,000 a month, then $2,000, $3,000, and ultimately $5,000 a month in real estate, stocks, bonds, etc.

Network Marketing can actually give you the access and the key to the vault in the other net worth-building investment models. Now your "extra few thousand a month" is worth a great deal more.

Geometric progression of your sales team's growth is easy to show on paper as a hypothetical but takes leadership, motivation, and dedicated effort for years to accomplish. Most people (an understatement) do not maintain their motivation to continue.

CHAPTER EIGHT

MOMENTUM

Insanity: Doing the same thing over and over again
and expecting different results.

– ALBERT EINSTEIN

Launching a Network Marketing sales group is much like pushing a car over a very slight hill. Imagine that you ran out of gas as you were driving up a hill. At the top of the hill the road becomes flat for some period of time and then slightly descends to the bottom of the hill where there is a gas station. Your mission is to get out of the car, get it rolling up the slight hill, to the top, and keep it going on the flat section until you crest the hill. Then you hop in and go for the ride of your life.

Network Marketing is the same. In the beginning, you will exert the most amount of effort promoting the product and enrolling new people for the least amount of return. Once you get things rolling, it will take less effort, but you must still keep pushing to keep it going. Once you gain momentum, you just hop in and enjoy the ride.

Momentum happens at different times in different companies. You will know it when you are in it. You will not be able to keep up with the requests people have for you, and your group will be on fire.

Going back to the car analogy, think of it like starting out pushing a Smart Car up the hill, then having it turn into a Cadillac at the top, and then into a Ferrari at the downhill crest.

It is the low return on effort in the beginning that leads most people to give up. They do not have the Vision and belief in the payoffs on the other side.

Another way to look at the growth of your group is to look at the Penny a Day chart on page 56. If it took a lot of effort to double that penny, given the return on investment of effort, most people would quit. Even halfway through the month, it is only worth $163.84! Yet if you

Critical Mass
Your Income
Becomes Residual

You Have Got The Ball
Rolling But... (2-4 years)

Launching Your
Business (1-2 years)

Get In And
Enjoy The Ride

Less Effort But You
Still Cannot Let Off

Maximum Effort
For Least Results

understand the power of Geometric Progression and compounding, then you KNOW if you keep doubling it, that little penny is worth over $5 million at the end of the month.

Day 1	$0.01	Day 16	$327.68
Day 2	$0.02	Day 17	$655.36
Day 3	$0.04	Day 18	$1,310.72
Day 4	$0.08	Day 19	$2,621.44
Day 5	$0.16	Day 20	$5,242.88
Day 6	$0.32	Day 21	$10,485.76
Day 7	$0.64	Day 22	$20,971.52
Day 8	$1.28	Day 23	$41,943.04
Day 9	$2.56	Day 24	$83,886.08
Day 10	$5.12	Day 25	$167,772.16
Day 11	$10.24	Day 26	$335,544.32
Day 12	$20.48	Day 27	$671,088.64
Day 13	$40.96	Day 28	$1,342,177.28
Day 14	$81.92	Day 29	$2,684,354.56
Day 15	$163.84	Day 30	$5,368,709.12

After 30 days, 1 penny becomes over 5 million dollars!

Geometric progression of your sales team's growth is easy to show on paper as a hypothetical but takes leadership, motivation, and dedicated effort for years to accomplish. Most people (an understatement) do not maintain their motivation to continue.

CHAPTER NINE

THE RENAISSANCE OF THE FAMILY & COMMUNITY

It's what you learn after you know it all that really counts.

– COACH JOHN WOODEN

Yes, it is true that building a sales organization of on-fire volunteers is still a challenge. However, it is being done, and in a powerful way. The biggest challenge is in erasing people's negative beliefs and biases about the Network Marketing concept and replacing them with what those of us who have already done it know to be true. And, it's coming. One day soon, world consciousness will shift and many people—perhaps most people—will in some way be a part of this dynamic, wealth-building industry.

Opportunity appreciation is not the only factor fueling the future of Network Marketing. It is also fueled by people's basic need to connect with others, to be a part of something bigger than themselves, and to have a sense of community.

Most of us know all too well that the family has disintegrated in many segments of our country. Since family is the foundation of neighborhoods and communities, they too have been compromised. Most of the industrialized world is deeply entrenched in the rat race—parents with full-time careers, day care, career advancement, soccer, music lessons, e-mail, social media, cell phones, payments, payments, and more payments. Some of us are winning the race, but as it's been said, "We are still rats!"

Today, people are longing for a return to a real, safe, relaxed time of freedom and soulful connection with others. People want to play together, pray together, get to really know each other, and most importantly, be known by others.

We want to improve ourselves, to have more pride in ourselves, to love and respect ourselves. We are hungry for guidance and support that will help us grow to be more powerful, more generous, and more self-assured. Anyone who has come full circle can tell you that these are the things that bring true happiness.

Achieving financial success and status is wonderful, especially if the alternative is being financially strapped to a life of despair. I think we'd all be better off rich, but money is relative—the more you have, the more you think you need.

Or, as it has been said, "Money is relative. The more money you have, the more relatives you have." There is a point, however, where we must have the wisdom to know when enough is enough.

This return to basic human values in business is a subtle, yet powerful, force driving the Network Marketing industry.

These are the qualities that will endear you to your family and to the community you create:

Patience	**Honesty**	**Forthrightness**
Generosity	**Integrity**	**Leadership**
Open-mindedness	**Authenticity**	**Love**
Cooperation	**Courage**	**Listening**

Network Marketing may offer the most dynamic environment for us to develop our spirituality, while managing our humanity at the same time. It may just be the most exciting leadership and character development program you have ever imagined. Are you up for that?

CHAPTER TEN

WHAT TO LOOK FOR IN A NETWORK MARKETING COMPANY

A building has integrity just like a man. And just as seldom.

– AYN RAND

1. Product

You must find a product or service you absolutely love, something you would:

- Buy forever, regardless of whether or not you are a Distributor.
- Recommend to others without reservation.

If you have to try to feel this way about the product, let it go. It will not work for you long term. Less important (but still vital) is that the product or service is consumable, which means that the customer will want to reorder it regularly.

Look at a list of billion dollar companies and look at what kinds of products they sell. Ask yourself … will this product really be relevant 25 years from now? Will it be in demand? Will it still be able to be competitively priced? Technology and service products are challenged here, as are commodities. Choose your product line with an eye on the long term. How long term? How long do you want to get paid? I prefer forever.

2. The Company

You must be proud of and trust the company and its leaders. They are your partners in product development, legal and financial issues, human resources, customer service, product development, order fulfillment, data processing, international expansion, public relations, ethics, and culture. They are crucial to your long-term success.

Imagine working hard for two or three years to build a solid Network

Marketing group, then having the company go out of business or embarrass you and your group so badly that everyone wants to quit.

Do your homework. Study the ownership and management of the company. Study the product's actual performance with customers. Study the compensation plan so you know ahead of time if it's something that will motivate and reward you. Most people spend more time analyzing a $50 Network Marketing product for purchase than they do the company when they decide to jump in and stake their reputations on it. Measure twice, cut once.

3. Your Upline

These are the people above you in your line of sponsorship. They will be partnering with you, training you, and supporting you. You will be spending countless hours with them. They may be in your home, and you in theirs. *You may be earning them a lot of money.* You must at least like them. Preferably you will love, honor, and respect them.

Look for people who are dedicated, loyal, focused, positive, committed, generous, and successful. And most importantly, once you choose your sponsor and upline, listen to them. Follow their lead. Get trained by them. Be coachable. They can only be successful if you are successful.

4. Follow Your Intuition, Find a Fit for Your Values

You're encouraged to use this book as the beginning of your Network Marketing education. Be a student. Do your homework. Start by talking frankly with whoever had the Vision and courage to give you this book.

If you can, find the right product, company, and people for you. If you can't, keep looking. Don't settle by copping out or by looking for reasons why it won't work. Instead, look with the intention of finding the right match—no matter how long it takes or what it requires of you.

When you find a company to call home, build your empire. Don't be deterred by challenges and setbacks, even dumb mistakes your company may make. Stick with them through thick and thin. Your life and the lives of thousands may be enriched. The world is waiting ...

SUCCESS STORIES

The following stories feature people who may be much like you. Certainly in the beginning, they didn't understand or necessarily believe in the possibilities of Network Marketing. And as you will read, most were not instant successes. Many of them have the same stories as most people during their first few months or even years … "This doesn't work!"

Yet, if you can reflect on the examples of duplication, compounding, and the car over the hill, it might help you make sense of these massive success stories. This is a much bigger opportunity than most people believe. And that is the promise of Network Marketing … that it is just an opportunity. What you do with it is up to you.

These stories are a sample of people I know who have made it big in Network Marketing and did it in an ethical and responsible manner in companies of the same character.

DISCLAIMER

These success stories are exceptional exceptions and are shared here to inspire you and show you people from different walks of life who have succeeded. They are not what you should expect to accomplish. They are 1 out of 10,000 or less. And yet it is interesting to note where they came from and what they accomplished. And maybe, just maybe, you could do the same.

HEATHER & WADE DOLL

RED DEER, ALBERTA, CANADA
LEADING THEIR TEAM BY EXAMPLE

Heather and Wade live in Red Deer, Alberta, and have been involved with Young Living since January 2013. Heather was dealing with tension headaches, and Wade was suffering with two ruptured discs and in a lot of pain. After trying other avenues without any success, they tried some oils and could not believe how much they helped!

Since January 2013, Heather and Wade have grown their organization to well over 8,000 members with a six figure monthly volume.

Heather and Wade's organization now exceeds 8,000 members (only 45 of those are personally enrolled), with their annual sales approaching $5,000,000. After enrolling, they achieved Silver within 41 days and Diamond 19 months later! The secret to their success has always involved being there for the team and running their business ethically.

Heather is a servant-driven leader, who travels often to help empower people in running their own events.

"Yes" is her favorite word! Heather has learned that events are very important to attend, and to become successful, you must be coachable. By focusing on keeping their home events simple and duplicable using a script Heather created for her team, they have experienced great duplication in their organization. Building
leadership and empowering members to become independent are very important to the Doll's organization.

Heather and Wade are continually educating themselves in regards to products, business, and personal growth. They have realized the importance of having family support in growing their business. Their three kids, Payton, Quinn, and Alexa, all love the oils; and Alexa, who is 7, loves to hang out with Mom at her "oil events"! The kids know there are sacrifices; however, they also understand and appreciate the bonus in having their parents at home and involved in their daily life!

Young Living has such wonderful products that it is easy to share them! Heather and Wade also love the fact that Young Living embraces Wellness, Purpose, and Abundance! If you have the will and determination, you can do this business too!

JAMIE & CHELSEA FLAMAN

RED DEER, ALBERTA, CANADA
FOUND FINANCIAL STABILITY WITH YOUNG LIVING

After using and loving the products, the business naturally followed. Jamie and Chelsea now have a team of over 10,000 members that grows by 500 members per month.

Life's most precious commodity is time. No matter how successful, rich or famous you are, you cannot simply buy more. For Chelsea, working as a full-time teacher with young children at home left very little time to savor the sweet moments and give back to others. She was "surviving," and like many jobs, working harder would not lead to a dramatic pay raise or a chance to "get ahead."

Even with two full-time, higher-than-average paying government jobs, Chelsea and Jamie found themselves struggling to climb out of debt. They couldn't imagine how Chelsea could realize her dream to stay home with their young family and pour her teaching efforts into homeschooling their own children.

After being introduced to Young Living Essential Oils, Chelsea quickly realized what a unique and needed product she had discovered. She found herself telling everyone she knew about these amazing oils, but didn't seriously consider the business until she received her first commission check.

She started hosting regular information sessions and focused on helping new members get their first few sign-ups. Within two years, she and Jamie hit and maintained the rank of Diamond, more than replacing two generous full-time salaries. That allowed Jamie to retire from his career and join Chelsea at home in growing the business and raising their four young children.

With over 500 members joining their Oil Culture team each month, and many passionate individuals continuing to share and empower others to do the same, they are consistently producing monthly sales in the six-figure range.

Duplication is very powerful considering that, of their 10,000+ team members, only around 100 were personally enrolled. With 350+ members sharing with new people each month, their numbers are climbing substantially.

Chelsea says: "When you have a passion for what you are doing, the motivation to succeed, and a product that people truly NEED, growth is inevitable. I believe Young Living is the best Network Marketing company. We have a product people desperately NEED at a time when people are seeking healthy alternatives at an unprecedented rate. I love that by empowering others to take care of their health, I get to stay home with my children and help others find financial freedom as well!"

Chelsea and Jamie hope that Young Living can be a means to a greater end as they consider what it means to be good stewards. They dream of the day when they can give far more than they keep and use their financial freedom and time to bless and serve others.

This success story is not typical and is shared to inspire you and show you what's possible. It is not what you should expect to accomplish.

CARLA & BILL GREEN

ROCKY MOUNTAIN HOUSE, ALBERTA, CANADA
MLM = MAKING LIVES MAGICAL

Carla and Bill Green are practitioners at their physical therapy, acupuncture and holistic health clinic, founded in 1985 in Rocky Mountain House, Alberta, Canada.

At the 2000 World Natural Medicine Conference, Carla met her mentor, Dr. Carolyn DeMarco. Dr. DeMarco introduced Carla to the amazing treatment effects of Young Living essential oils. As a pediatric acupuncture specialist, when Carla heard how these oils could help all her patients, especially "her kids," she was hooked!

Carla and Bill's "Team Inukshuk" is fast approaching 40,000 members (180 personally enrolled), adding 2,500 new members per month, with $2,000,000 in sales per month.

Being the consummate researcher, Carla began looking at why these oils worked in the human body. She discovered they stimulated the pituitary hypothalamus axis in the brain, the same part of the brain stimulated by acupuncture, which she trusted. "I was intrigued," Carla said. "Could essential oils act like acupuncture in a bottle?"

Carla began successfully using oils on her family. She was soon trying them on her long-term patients. "I chose the essential oil that matched their complaint and applied it to the soles of their feet before their acupuncture treatment. If they suffered insomnia, I applied lavender; if they had a cold, I applied Thieves," states Carla. Of those patients, 100% said it "was the best treatment they EVER had."

Carla transitioned out of using traditional Chinese herbs, replacing them with essential oils. In 2005, Carla and Bill developed their Second Chance Facial Rejuvenation protocol. Needing topical and nutritional products, the only choice was Young Living.

"Originally, we hid the business aspect, as 'MLM' was a bad word! We simply offered people a way to purchase wholesale for their personal use," says Bill.

Through voracious sharing, they "accidently" won the 2007 Young Living incentive cruise, which changed their lives and their opinion of MLM.

Networking with other successful Young Living leaders, and not trying to "recreate the wheel" of success, paved the way for their business momentum. "We loved the fact that no matter what your income or background, if you were willing to acquire the easy-to-learn skills of network marketing, you could have an equal opportunity for financial success!"

Today their "Team Inukshuk" is fast approaching 40,000 members (180 personally enrolled), adding 2,500 new members per month, with $2,000,000 in sales per month.

MLM now means "Making Lives Magical," and Carla and Bill's story proves it does not matter when you embrace the business aspect and learn the needed skills; once you do, magic really does happen!

This success story is not typical and is shared to inspire you and show you what's possible. It is not what you should expect to accomplish.

ADAM GREEN

LAKE COUNTY, BRITISH COLUMBIA, CANADA
**TREAT YOUR BUSINESS LIKE A BUSINESS,
GET PAID LIKE A BUSINESS**

By treating his business like a business, Adam was able to "retire" at age 22. Now, five years later, Adam's team has more than 35,000 members and exceeds $1,500,000 in sales monthly.

At age 11, Adam's mom introduced him to Young Living products, but he didn't understand there was a business plan attached. In their family, natural products, such as essential oils, were familiar. It's simply what they used!

During college, Adam hit the low point of his life … living for the weekend and partying to escape reality. Nearing rock bottom, Adam discovered the power of the Network Marketing business model when his friend invited him to an opportunity meeting.

His first thoughts were, "WOW! How was I not taught about this in all my years of schooling, never taught or told about this as a viable career choice and profession?"

Hungry for more information, he attended a series of meetings of increasing size to learn what he could about this eye-opening business model. The ability to control his own destiny by being his own boss was very enticing, especially looking at retiring from traditional work in four years instead of forty! With his passion for natural health, Young Living Essential Oils was the perfect fit.

At first, Adam was building his Young Living business part time, as he worked as a full-time personal trainer. In late 2011, at 22 years old, Adam resigned from his job and committed full time to his business.

A mentor had taught him: "Treat your business like a business, get paid like a business. Treat your business like a hobby, and get paid like a hobby." With his resignation, Adam chose to engage in his Young Living business like the fantastic business opportunity it really was and began building a massive organization.

When he engaged, he personally sponsored 46 new people in the first year, along with 37 the next year, 45 the year after that, and 29 people the following year.

With that shift, five years later, Adam's team has grown from 250 people to more than 35,000! At only 27 years old, Adam leads an organization with $1,500,000 in monthly sales and growing. Adam wrote his first book *25 to Life: Jailbreak Your 9-5 & Escape to Financial Freedom* to inspire more millennials to take control of their financial futures through Network Marketing.

Adam has found his purpose and is living a lifestyle that many only dream about. Adam's burning desire to share the value of this profession and empower others with their physical and financial health is infectious among his dedicated "Green Team" members.

Connie Marie McDanel

BEMIDJI, MINNESOTA, USA
SUCCESS IS A PATTERN

As a passionate EntreprenOILer, Connie's team consists of some of Young Living's best-trained distributors. They produce over $50 million volume annually and their momentum continues to welcome 5000+ new members each month.

Connie had a fulfilling career as a teacher, yet her passion and commitment didn't create the security she wanted for her own family. Every year she faced budget cuts or district downsizing, which left her uncertain about whether she would have a job. She dreamed of a business where she could contribute to the greater good, have the security she wanted in life, and be in control of her own time.

After the loss of young family members to cancer and prescription drugs, Connie's passion rose. She realized that Young Living was a way to contribute something meaningful to people's lives and create security for her own family. Her strong belief in the value that Young Living products provided to individuals and families made it natural for her to recommend them to others.

Through FOCUSED activity and the vision to see what her organization could become, Connie resigned from teaching early and became a stay-at-home parent. She loves being able to educate others about the physical and financial possibilities of Young Living. Watching other families get out of debt and build a LEGACY of prosperity is incredibly rewarding.

Connie has now been instrumental in changing the legacies of thousands of families across the globe while earning a place in the Million Dollar Earners Club. Her team produces over $50 million volume annually and their team's momentum continues to welcome 5000+ new members each month.

Connie believes that success IS a pattern and the key is to teach this pattern to others. In her 17 years in the business, she has personally enrolled around 200 members, giving them a shining example of the power of duplication. She has helped others to dream beyond a traditional career income simply by recommending the amazing benefits of Young Living.

She has great respect for her strong team of EntreprenOILers. With the enhancement of technology and third party tools, her group has accelerated traditional income success into 3-5 years. Connie concludes, "Life is TOO short to continue trading time for money. Families are looking for options and a way to fulfill their 'someday' dreams! Let's do this TOGETHER!"

VICKI OPFER

PARKER, COLORADO, USA
CREATING ABUNDANCE THROUGH BEING OF SERVICE

With a group of over 85,000 active members in over 120 countries, Vicki has the freedom to do what she enjoys – helping people discover how to live healthier and happier lives!

In 1994, Vicki was introduced to Young Living Essential Oils by her daughter, Jessica, who was 15 and wanted an oils kit. When Vicki realized that Young Living was a network marketing company, she was resistant to enrolling and had no interest in building a business.

After experiencing the profound effect of essential oils on the health and wellness of her family and friends, Vicki made a personal commitment to share the products with as many people as possible. Through the dedication of many like-minded people in her organization, two years later, Vicki became the second Diamond in Young Living.

In the years since, Vicki has developed a deep respect for the network marketing business model. Her goal has been to use the MLM model to create a thriving business "with integrity and without hype or pressure to sell."

Vicki is helping to create a new paradigm in the MLM industry, where distributors focus on genuinely helping others through sharing Young Living's life-changing products in a duplicable way.

She says, "This business model offers everyday people the opportunity to create amazing abundance while doing what they love. It's an extraordinary way to experience life!"

Vicki's book *Harmony, Joy, and Abundance* is a primer on sharing Young Living, and has been used by many leaders throughout Young Living to teach and model the skills required for duplication and success.

Vicki says, "The key to success is simple: Help the members of your organization share the Young Living lifestyle with their friends and families in a genuine, effective, and duplicable way, so that many people, worldwide, can live healthier, happier, and more abundant lives."

YL Family, Inc. is a multigenerational family business and Vicki considers all 85,000 members of her organization to be her extended family. She is extraordinarily grateful and humbled to work with her "family" each and every day.

MELISSA POEPPING

Melissa traded in long hours and little pay owning a daycare for independence and success!

After 2 short years of owning a daycare, Melissa realized that working 60 hours per week and making $16,800 per year was not for her. Having spent years in sales and finance, this Minnesota girl knew she needed something more. *But what option would allow her and her husband, Wayne, to raise their children, earn 6 figures and work from home?*

In the summer of 2010, Melissa asked her sponsor of 10 years to show her how to build a Young Living Business! Her sponsor was shocked because up until that point, Melissa had shown no interest in having "one of those MLM businesses."

Energy, vitality, health, happiness, feeling rested and full of life! The health benefits Melissa and her family were experiencing with Young Living were PHENOMENAL, and she felt obligated to share this resource with others!

Her sponsor's suggestion: home parties.

Melissa's response: "NO! I don't KNOW anyone! I live in a SMALL town of 76 people in the country! I have NEVER done this before! What will people THINK?! What will my husband and my friends think?!"

Less than a week later, Melissa had a "Young Living Home Experience Kit" in her hands. As soon as the home experience gatherings were underway, her team started growing! They were providing information that, they soon found out, was being craved in their community! In no time at all, they had created a movement that was quickly catching on!

Showing others how to create a Young Living lifestyle impacts generations to come and allows them to take control of their wellness, and if they so choose, their economy!

In just 4 years, while working from home and raising their 3 children, Melissa reached financial independence. She went from 12 members to over 13,000 with teams in 5 countries … a true Four Year Career success!

Today she has nearly 18,000 members across the world as a Crown Diamond with Young Living. With the success of duplication, Melissa continues to experience phenomenal business each year while producing over $1MM in volume each month.

Melissa has personally sponsored and enrolled just 43 members. The success of "The Sweet Team" is the result of team effort. Melissa feels she has an unstoppable group of strong leaders with a contagious passion and desire to share!

Her message to entrepreneurs just starting out? Don't let your circumstances define you, focus on what you REALLY want to create in your life, and let the thought of limitations dissolve.

Wellness, purpose and abundance await you!

This success story is not typical and is shared to inspire you and show you what's possible. It is not what you should expect to accomplish.

Rob & Alina Rinato

SARASOTA, FLORIDA, USA
GOODBYE DEBT, HELLO RESIDUAL INCOME

In just 18 months, Rob and Alina replaced their income and reached a six-figure residual income ... all before age 30.

In 2009, Rob and Alina were hardworking massage therapists living in upstate New York. After paying their bills each month, they consistently found themselves in a place many young adults do: just over broke with mountains of debt and no time or energy left to enjoy their lives. It was clear – something needed to change.

When one of Rob's clients approached him about using Young Living, he wasn't interested initially, but he knew Alina would be, as she was into natural health. Alina attended a workshop and fell in love with the oils.

Her interest was truly piqued when she heard about the chance to win a free cruise. Despite his skepticism of the products and Network Marketing, Rob agreed to order the Everyday Oils and the NingXia Red because of Alina's excitement.

They were both amazed at the results they had with their own health! After only a few weeks of using and diffusing the oils, it was clear the Young Living lifestyle was for them.

Realizing how many other people were looking for natural options, it was an obvious choice to begin sharing and teaching about Young Living. Their sponsor said to them, "Even if it takes you 10 years of part-time work to earn $10,000 a month in residual income, wouldn't it be worth it?"

With that in mind, they set out to build their business part-time while learning as much as they could about Network Marketing. They discovered that teaching others to teach others is more important than making sales. This one distinction helped the couple grow their business to where it replaced their income in 18 months and earned them a six-figure residual income by their third year – all before the age of 30.

Today their team consists of over 12,000 members and enrolls over 500 new members every month. Their growing organization produces over $5 million dollars in annual sales. "In only a few short years we were able to permanently solve our financial problems and radically change our lifestyle."

Rob and Alina are honored to be part of a profession that's all about paying it forward. With the help of their incredible, dedicated team, they will continue to empower others with the message of Wellness, Purpose, and Abundance with Young Living.

DEBRA RAYBERN

MONTGOMERY, TEXAS, USA
SIX FIGURES IN DEBT TO SIX FIGURE INCOME

From personal and financial tragedy to more than enough for Debra and her family.

As a certified nutritional counselor, Master Herbalist, naturopath, and aromatherapist, Debra owned a successful wellness consulting business that was more for hobby than full-time income. While teaching a class on herbs, Debra was introduced to Young Living Essential Oils in March 2000 by a student. Previously unimpressed with essential oils from other companies, Debra knew immediately these Young Living essentials oils were different and she needed to incorporate them into her business.

As the essential oils took care of family health issues, friends came to learn and they brought their friends, which laid a foundation of 99 members.

She was not interested in building a Young Living business because according to her, she didn't really understand the MLM model. Then the unexpected death of her husband in 2002 left her six figures in debt and in need of a greater income. Not wanting to sacrifice time with daughter Sharon, whom she was home schooling, she began praying for an answer. In the summer of 2005 the answer she received from God was "I gave you the oils." She began calling her 99 members to set up classes.

Of the nearly 40 people who attended one of her first classes, all enrolled in Young Living. It was a sign to her that Young Living was indeed her answer to her prayer. She continued teaching 2-3 classes nearly every week for two years. Debra suggests others find out what they are good at and use those talents to share the Young Living message of Wellness, Purpose, and Abundance. "You are the one who makes you successful, so no matter your style, use the products, share the opportunity, and Just Do It!"

After personally enrolling over 300 members, with many months exceeding 20,000 new members, her team now has over 260,000 members and exceeds $100 million in annual sales and no slow down in sight.

Debra is truly grateful to God for bringing Young Living into her life. With Young Living she works from anywhere, has the flexibility to set her own hours, and has a business growing 24/7—even while she sleeps. She also has a great group of associates and friends to work with and the ability to help more people than she ever could imagine. Debra retired from her consulting business to share with even more people.

This success story is not typical and is shared to inspire you and show you what's possible. It is not what you should expect to accomplish.

Dr. Scott & Brenda Schuler

OAK PARK, MINNESOTA, USA
**ESCAPED THE RAT RACE, NOW WORKING
SMARTER NOT HARDER**

Scott and Brenda have built an organization of over 56,000 members and are growing by over 4,500 new members each month.

Scott and Brenda were born and raised in Minnesota. Scott, a chiropractor, and Brenda, an Exercise Physiologist, were both groomed in the philosophy of the traditional "job."

In 1999, a co-worker introduced Brenda to Young Living to aid in her digestive issues. Disillusioned by a previous Network Marketing experience, Brenda only used Young Living's incredible products for herself and her family. Not understanding the Network Marketing opportunity, they believed in and shared the product, but Scott refused to let Brenda share with friends and family because it was Network Marketing. In 2008, after the birth of their third son, Scott watched as Brenda's checks continued to rise and passion changed. He made the decision to "fire" her from his chiropractic clinic and encouraged her to follow her newly found passion with Young Living.

As Brenda began treating her passion as a career, she realized just like any other profession, there were skills needed. Brenda embarked on a knowledge quest to find how to professionally and successfully pursue Network Marketing. Scott and Brenda maintain personal self-development, which is key to their continued success. After all, "readers are leaders and learners are earners."

Putting in 10-12 hour days, Scott enviously watched Brenda's freedom of time and income rise as he was stuck, even as a business owner, trading more time for less money. In 2010 Scott and Brenda made the decision to sell his part of the chiropractic clinic. Scott and Brenda's new partnership, one of two different but complementing personalities, has propelled their business forward to new heights.

Currently their organization is 56,000 members strong and averaging 4,500 new members a month. These numbers result in yearly sales well into the eight-figure range.

Scott and Brenda have coached and witnessed those who implemented the skills needed, regardless of their personal circumstances, become successful in Young Living. If you have the desire, commitment and willingness to apply what is taught, you too can achieve wellness, purpose, and abundance through Young Living.

They conclude, "We have been blessed with amazing, strong and dedicated leaders on our team and at the end of the day that is the true reason for our success."

DUANE & JILENE HAY

KELOWNA, BRITISH COLUMBIA, CANADA
FINDING FREEDOM TO LIVE THEIR TRUE CALLING

Duane and Jilene are now working full-time training, empowering, and supporting their team of more than 9,000 members.

Stay-at-home mom Jilene and cable installer Duane discovered Young Living at a home presentation in 2012. Right away, they found it easy to apply essential oils in their home and use for their children. As teething pains were soothed and the kids started sleeping better, Jilene thought of her Mom's sleep struggles and recommended she try the oils too!

There were so many "there's an oil for that!" conversations happening that Jilene and Duane began recommending Young Living easily and confidently. Soon the awesome testimonies started coming back from friends and family. It wasn't long before a small army of families who loved Young Living started to grow with the attitude "when you have something good, you have a responsibility to share it!"

A turning point came when Jilene attended a small event. She was struck with the idea that time is the only limited commodity. She left that night knowing she had an opportunity in front of her to make a big impact in people's lives.

"It made us stop and think closely about how we wanted to spend our time. Living life together as a family, being in community, loving others and giving back, that was what was important. We realized that Young Living was the opportunity we had been waiting for!"

Shortly after, Young Living launched their Silver in 6 Elite Express incentive. The potential prizes and earning opportunity sparked Duane and Jilene to approach their relationship with Young Living as a business.

They realized that their impact was limited by how many people they could personally help, but would be UNLIMITED if they could empower their team to help others. With this new outlook, they began intentionally recommending and inviting others to try Young Living as well as to share it. "We realized that everyone has a dream and a purpose in life. Too often we have turned off that side, because of circumstance or belief. We have found a way that opens the doors for people to begin dreaming again and create massive impact in their own lives and in the lives of those they care about."

Fueled by a burning desire to keep families healthy and whole, Duane and Jilene are now working full-time training, empowering and supporting their team of more than 9,000 members and 300+ business builders. Their amazing "Thrive Family Essentials" team is growing steadily with annual sales of over $6,000,000.

"Regardless of whether or not we ever made a dime sharing Young Living, we love the products so much that we would continue to use and recommend them to everyone! I think that has been crucial to our success. Passion that's contagious."

DISCLAIMER

These success stories are exceptional exceptions and are shared here to inspire you and show you people from different walks of life who have succeeded. They are not what you should expect to accomplish. They are 1 out of 10,000 or less. And yet it is interesting to note where they came from and what they accomplished. And maybe, just maybe, you could do the same.

Your income will depend entirely on you, your commitment, your work ethic, your leadership, and your ability to acquire customers and inspire sales leaders to join your team.

Most people who start off intending to build a sales team do not maintain their motivation to continue.

RICHARD BLISS BROOKE

Richard would love to hear your stories of how this work has impacted your life or business. You can reach Richard at 855.480.3585 or RB@BlissBusiness.com.

THE FOUR YEAR
CAREER®

SHARE IT

The Four Year Career® is a book to be shared. Your prospects are just like you, so why not use this to build your business? This proven prospecting tool is generic for any Network Marketing opportunity and can bring the shift in momentum you've been waiting for!

- **Makes prospecting easy.** Instead of YOU having to explain Network Marketing and residual income, the book does it for you!

- Allows you to stop selling. Once you give someone the book, it creates a **seamless transition** into talking about your own opportunity.

- Builds your prospects' belief, as well as the **belief of your new team members**. When teams are on the same page, amazing things happen!

> **For bulk discounts, visit:**
> **BLISSBUSINESS.COM/4YC**

CONNECT WITH RICHARD
ON FACEBOOK & THE WEB

There's so much to **LIKE** when you become a fan of Richard:

- Get Richard's top tips and insights on how to build your empire
- Enter to win free products (including Richard's bestselling books!)
- Interact with Richard and other industry pros who share your passions
- Be the first to know about upcoming events and the latest industry news
- Share your favorite posts to build belief and credibility in your opportunity
- Get inspired with Richard's videos, thought-provoking posts, and so much more

Richard is excited to connect with you on Facebook and help you along your journey to Network Marketing success. Become a fan today: **facebook.com/RichardBlissBrooke**

Visit his website at: **blissbusiness.com**

ALSO BY RICHARD BLISS BROOKE

- Step-by-step guide on how to break through your self-imposed limitations and program your subconscious mind to expect success
- Exercises to help you create your Vision and make it more vivid and powerfully imprinted
- Discover how to act powerfully and attract powerfully

"Congratulations! I just read your *Mach2* book, and it is a masterpiece … head and shoulders above the rest of the motivation books I have read."

HARVEY MACKAY
Chairman & Founder, MackayMitchell

"I love *Mach2*. I could tell when I read the book that Richard has a passion for changing people's lives. I respect Richard and his work and thank him for who he is and the difference and impact he's making in people's lives and businesses."

LES BROWN
Motivational Speaker

To learn more, visit:
BLISSBUSINESS.COM/MACH2